Copyright © 2022 Faten Hatem.

All rights reserved. No part of this publication may be reproduced, distributed, or transmitted in any form or by any means, including photocopying, recording, or other electronic or mechanical methods, without the prior written permission of the publisher, except in the case of brief quotations embodied in critical reviews and certain other noncommercial uses permitted by copyright law. For permission requests, write to the author. All photos used are collected from royalty-free websites and public domains unless they are personal pictures of the author.
The e-book version of the book is best viewed in landscape mode.

ISBN: 9798840120330

Printed by Amazon.

First printing edition 2022.

Dedication

To my parents, who always gave and never took...

To those whose care was present while everyone's humanity was absent...

To my best friends who are still there for me...

To all those who encouraged me and taught me...

To those who believed in me...

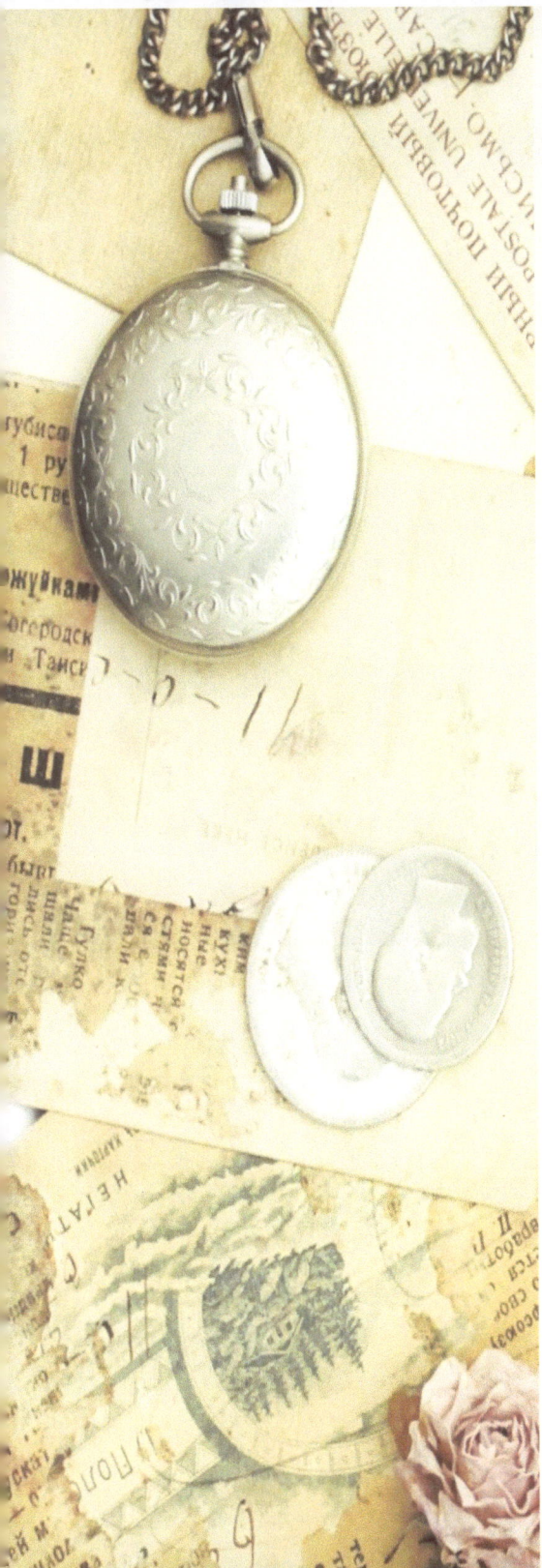

Like my father used to tell us...
"Seek knowledge even if it takes you to China"...

Ancient Arabic proverb

Faten Mostafa Hatem

Researcher, architect, and artist
Joint MA Heritage Conservation and Site Management;
BTU Cottbus-Senftenberg, Germany & Helwan University, Egypt
B.Sc. Architectural Engineering; Ain Shams University, Egypt
e-mail: fatenmostafahatem@gmail.com
https://fatenhatem092.wixsite.com/website

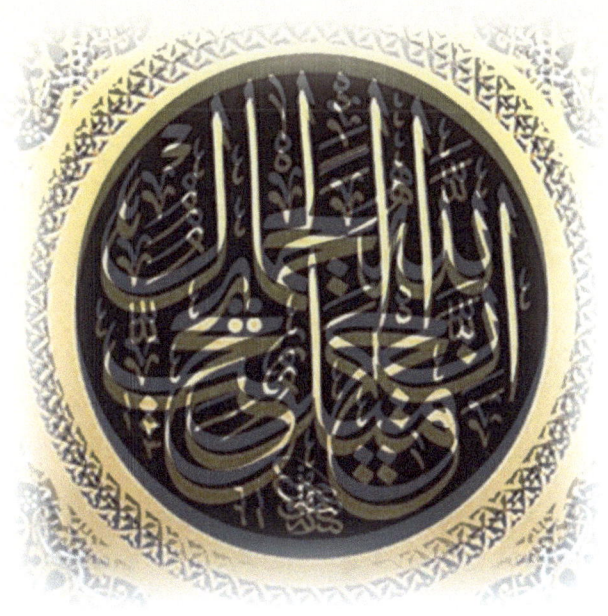

"Indeed, Allah is Beautiful, and loves beauty."

Hadith (a statement by Prophet Muhammad)

" 'Indeed, God is Beautiful' means that His alone is Absolute Beauty, comprising of the Beauty of His Essence, Attributes, and Actions. And by 'He loves beauty' what is meant is that God loves [actions such as] the beautifying one's person, rarely revealing one's needs to others, and safeguarding the honor of others." Sh. al-Munawi (d. 1621)

www.thesilsila.com

Bringing smart cities back to people

In the era of speed, big data, and technology, one cannot help but notice how the focus on the growth of the city and becoming 'smart' has made it difficult to pay sufficient attention to the implications of such trends on people; the very element that has always been necessary for its existence and survival. The interaction between people and the different government and commercial sectors, as well as the ongoing occupation of the city, are two salient features of what a city even means, and yet, following a techno-computational logic the revolution of smart urbanization is heavily invested in the aim of enhancing basic functionalities while assuming such technological innovations will lead to more liveable cities and improve residents' experiences. Smart city visions rarely pinpoint the scope, dimensions, or 'the how' of intended effects, whereas, in reality, the smart city reveals the truth of mixed outcomes and failures to fulfil claimed potentials. As an architect who has lived in four different cities in three continents for long periods of time, I have experienced the powerful effects and affects of architecture in my personal daily life.

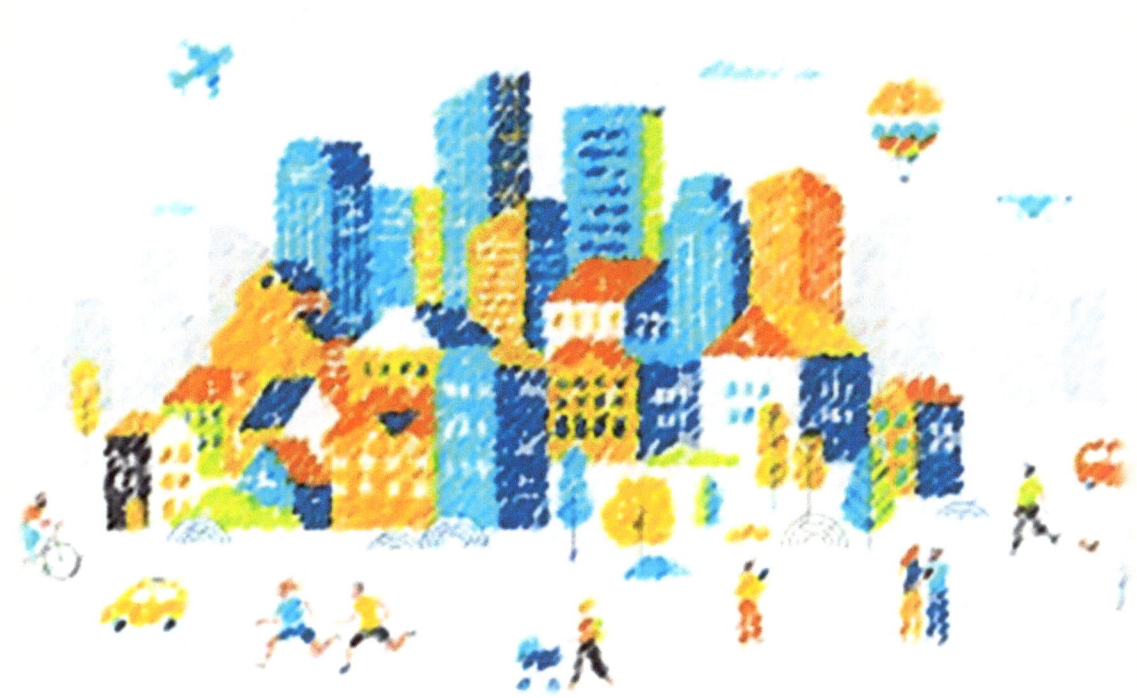

I find it difficult to live with many architects' pre-occupation with the pleasure of the eye and their often wilful neglect of other senses to the extent that this stance has become naturalized and embodied in the modern architectural design practice, leaving human beings unsatisfied, detached and unengaged by imbalanced experiences that focus namely on one sense. For cities, it is almost the exact difference between a house and home, as one is a physical building; the other a place of comfort, protection, and memories, a shelter where we belong. For a smart city to actually be smart, it has to value and empower people; it has to shed the understanding that disregarding human nature and its inherent needs is not smart; and it has to gain an awareness of the fact that shallow experiences have insufficient power to motivate people, to make them stay for long, dwell in and revisit places and create lasting good impressions in their minds. Thus there is a need to develop new design principles, frameworks, and practices that redefine smart urbanization through dialogues amongst corporates, governors, design professionals, and communities; that challenge the singular focus of smart city developments away from instrumental rationalities (installing high technologies in the smart city) embodied in functionalities and attempt to reinstate values-based rationalities (practical wisdom) and human experiences.

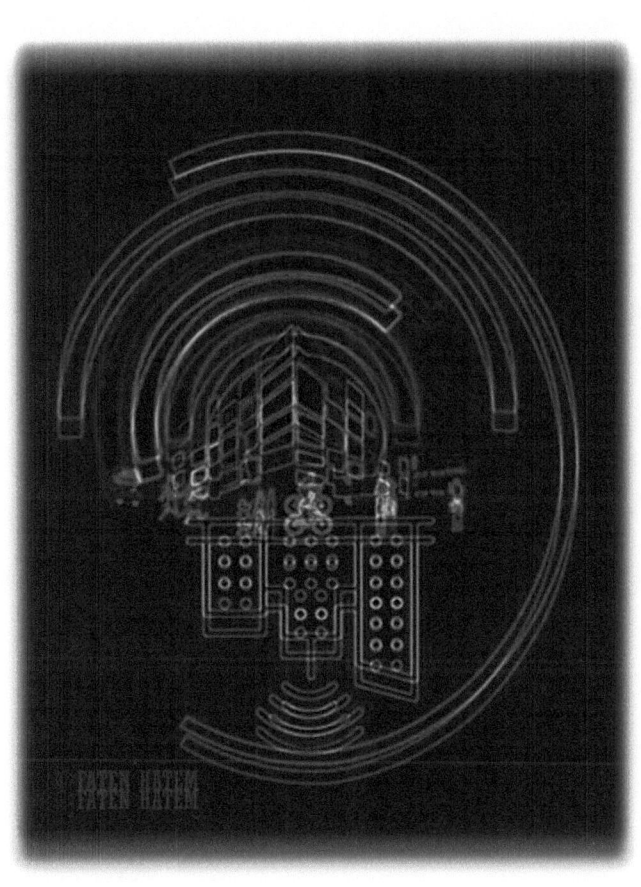

To create a truly smart design, it is important to make this transition from an embodied practice to a more reflective practice where the overlooked inherent need for a sense of belonging as well as the "existential need to feel rooted in time as much as in space"-as in Pallasmaa`s words-are finally acknowledged and fulfilled. This also means that even homogeneous perspectives and assumptions of what constitutes a good architectural (and planning) practice can be challenged, preferably by the practitioners themselves. Such changes are necessary to create and maintain better sense of place, foster responsibility for public participation, and help attain long-term sustainability, resulting in successful and authentic smart cities.

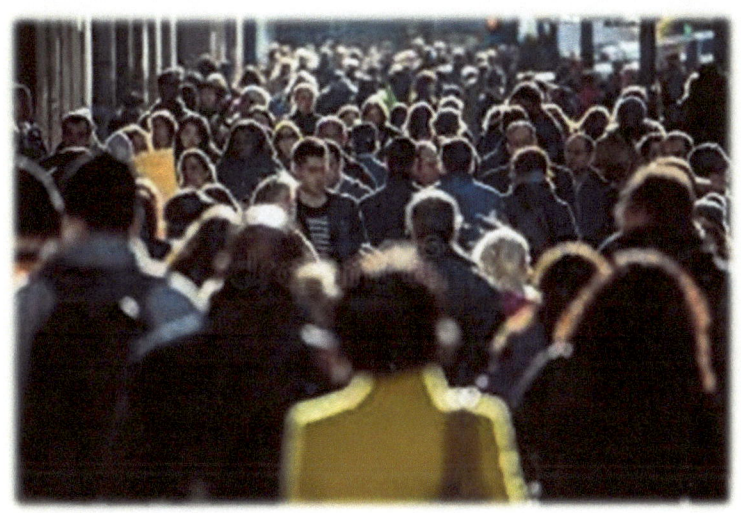

Excruciatingly Beautiful

I couldn't apologize...for making her cry. She was reading my poetry and I was there watching her body shivering, her eyes watering with tears and her voice choking more and more...by my words. She kept reading a poem, after a poem, unstoppably and I couldn't do anything but let her water that thirst. After finishing them all, she was quite happy..or maybe not happy, perhaps satisfied...or somehow calmed down after enjoying that relief, she was amazingly relieved by liberating that pain. That grounding sensation that art brings about by exposing wounds that were buried under the daily burdens of our busy lives, and letting you to some extent accept the nature of it, the reality of it...the beauty of it.

It is amazing how powerful lines, words, and objects can be when they are put together to tell us something, remind us of something...or even make us think and rethink something. How powerful they can be when they force us to see..oh, how scary they can be..when we confess to missing something, someone ... some..time. It is then that it feels like I am hiding from my own thoughts, hiding from that moment of wanting so much to cry..that cold feeling of loneliness, that unescapable train of memories..that dark and very beautiful corner that I can no longer be in, have or enjoy.

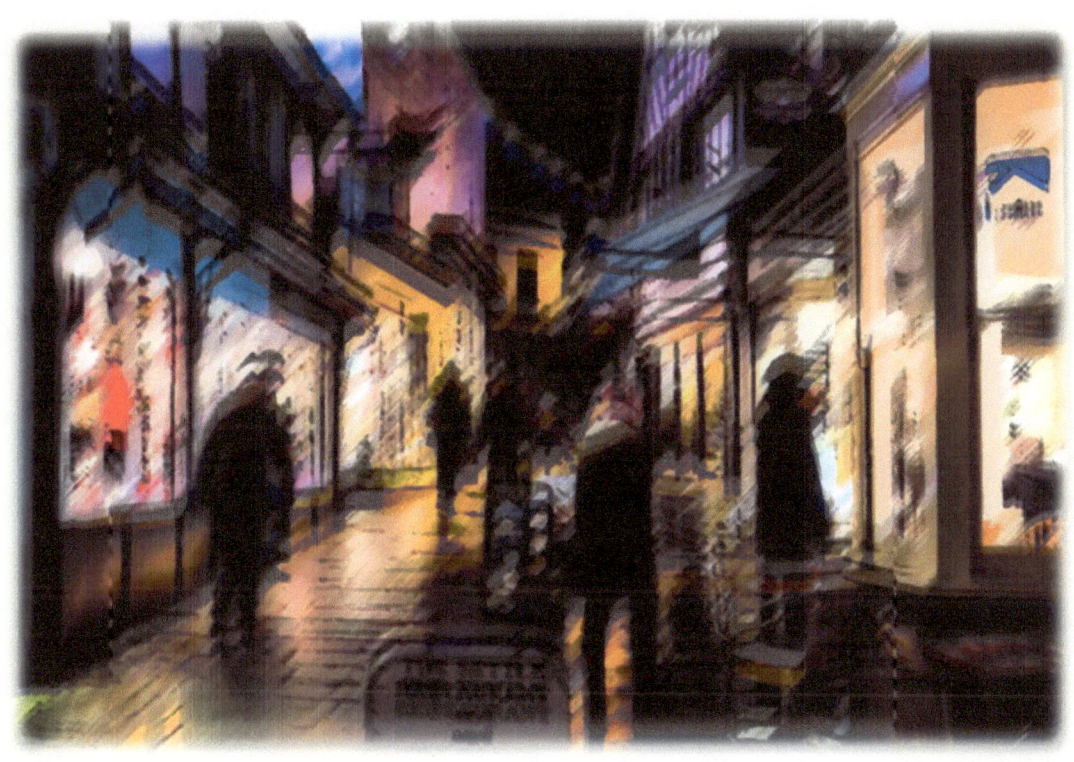

To those who experienced being away from home, they know how similar it is to actually miss someone you loved so long...so much..so..deeply. The thing is a place can reside in us just like we reside in it, it enclothes our bodies and souls and it is so powerful that engulfs your senses, your memory, and your emotions. Traveling around the world taught me so much about home and how a house is different from that safe shelter that I miss and hurry back to when I feel exhausted, afraid, or lonely. The sad thing is that there are places in which I lived for long periods of time, but I could not miss them, for they could not be homes to me. Similar to people, cities that reject the individual, make him feel unwelcomed, and even uncomfortable cannot be missed. They fall short of evoking that home sensation. Biologists say that missing something stems from the brain getting addicted to the triggers of happiness hormones. I do not disagree, getting used to that fix is the essence that makes us miss it. What I think is that getting used to the feeling of someone is what we cannot let go easily of. However, it is just one`s sense of safety that is assured by this addiction and it is endangered by leaving them or them leaving us. I have been to room viewings to live with other single ladies who told me they keep birds, music, and lights on to have a feeling of someone in the house. I know, I felt even sadder to hear that in person but isn't that why we have art, enjoy art and even make art too? To be with?

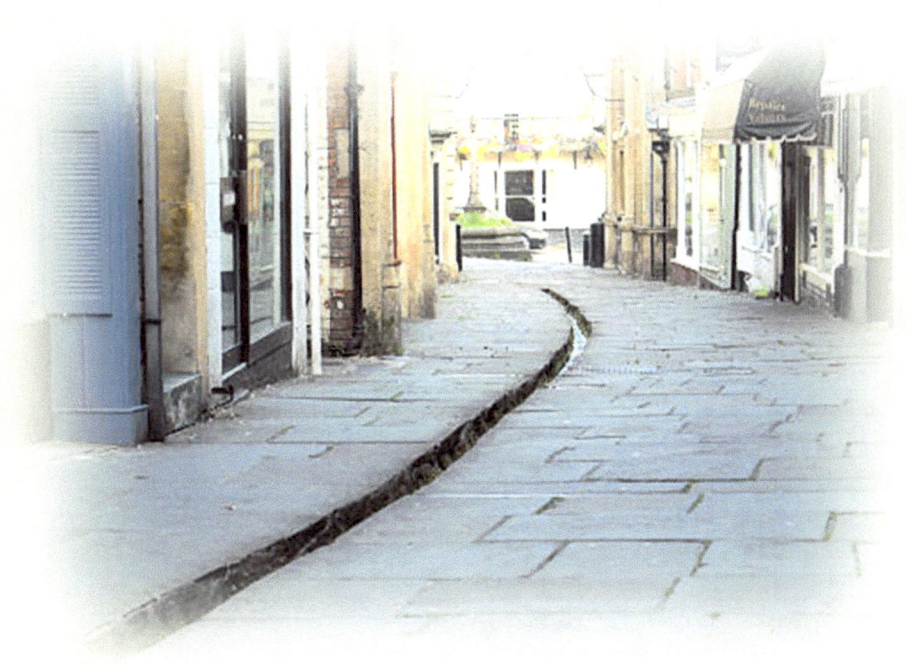

Various types of art communicate atmospheres of safety and danger very well that I think we as architects and researchers should listen to and maybe use to get better at delivering emotionally safe cities, cities that we miss; cities that will have people want to stay in them and make them prosper and flourish. That is a long-term sustainability approach that needs to be integrated with the eco-friendly, clean transportation and autonomous services that city planning and governance are highly focused on. One afternoon I was having my coffee in one of the central squares in Glasgow, I was enjoying the view in front of me sculptures, ancient buildings and clean streets. I looked back to check the view from in the other direction, to my surprise I was quite happy just to notice the light traffic, the stream of people going further, and some others taking pictures of their friends. The same feeling came to me when I was in Airdrie, a very simple and small city but those streets going up to see some distinct seagulls flying, mountains gracefully wrapped up in fog and a few rose trees around some houses that I enjoy smelling on my way every day. The main landmarks I could see are memorials of people who lived there, made the city and lost their lives for a cause or war that you see residents leaving flowers and items showing their love, respect and belonging. Other people, I see waving to each other through glass and customers and sellers calling each other by name and others joking with me.

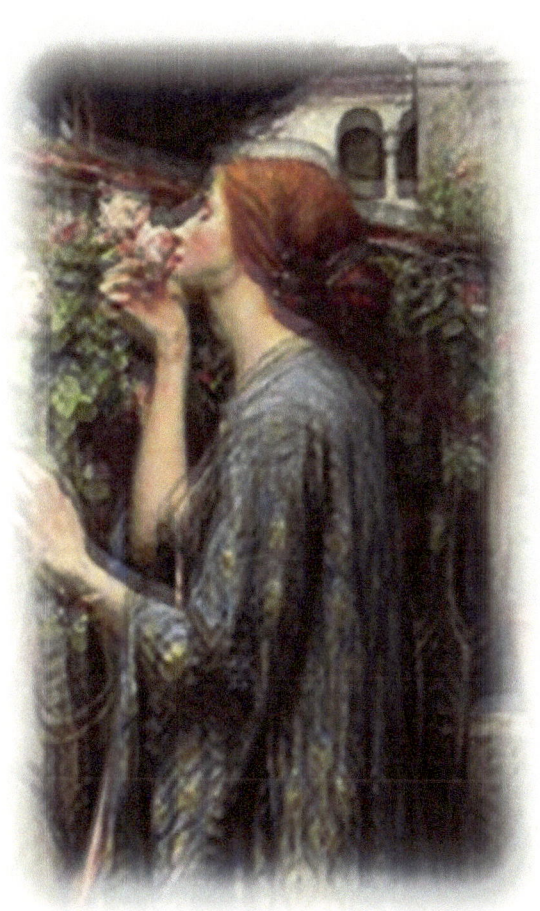

That sensation of being surrounded by that feeling of companionship made me smile while sadly realizing that I missed my friends and family, the people in our neighborhood myself self and ...my home. Then I realized that these cities that I could not miss, either don`t show that sense of welcoming community or personalization or sometimes don't even have a clear heart of the city like in Milton Keynes. From my experience, living in an impersonal place or a city works o in the other way around too. I remember when my friend explained to me once this theory about being out and being seen. It goes something like this, it feels better when you get out of the house basically because you are being visible and recognized. This appreciation of your existence, therefore, uplifts your feeling self-esteem esteem. I couldn't help but ask; could it be that I'm not visible in the big impersonal alien city that I feel sad about not being missed, myself?!

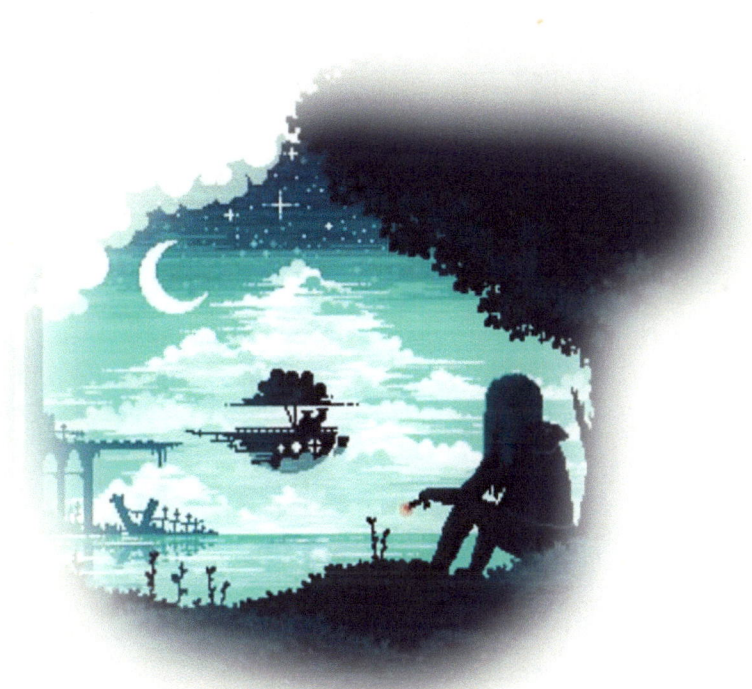

"The Beautiful Woman has Come"

It is not a strange scene to see all the visitors standing in amazement around the fascinating limestone sculpture of the queen which testifies for her beauty as much as her Egyptian birth name that means "The Beautiful Woman has Come". The bust of Nefertiti was not only carefully and skilfully sculpted using some stone and colours, but it is also showing the rare observation and understanding of an artist that knows that angles, shades and texture are just as important. The level of detail that the eye keeps discovering little by little as you revolve around the sculpture without ever being bored with is another testimony to how much the maker appreciated the viewer as much as he appreciated the beauty of a queen. A beauty that has been delicately represented as elegant and majestic yet compassionate at the same time. It is seldom that I come across an engaging work of art that I don't notice a consideration of shadows, movement and expressive details in it which makes you not only see something but also feel as well.

As an architect, I cannot stop myself comparing the way different forms of arts communicate with people and how much we are missing to learn, use and give enough time to consider.

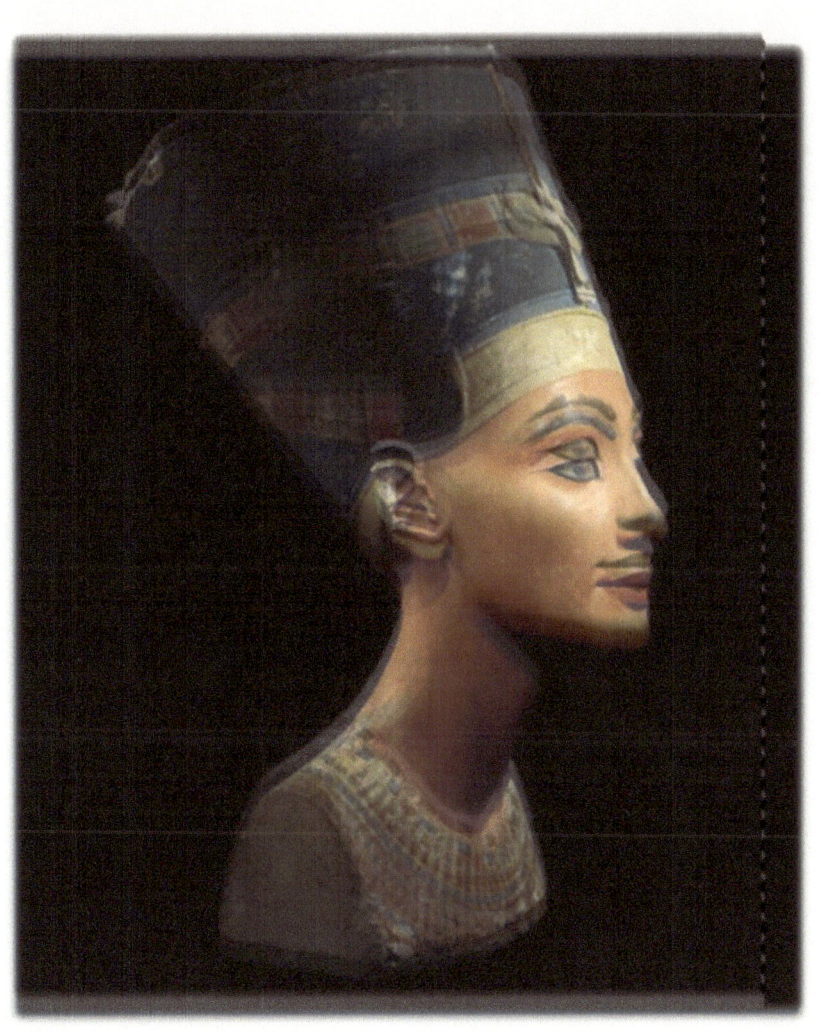

This is surely better done before we quickly fall in love with our charcoal hand sketches or even the computer-filtered images that are used mainly for marketing a product to the client. I am not against the tools themselves; it is just the knowledge and purpose standing behind them that always frightens me. I think it is dangerous, very dangerous to neglect the fact that we as humans are continuously affected by our surroundings.

On the other hand, it is not a completely surprising result to find this rush to produce an iconic shape of a building in architecture studios and faculties that have studied and honoured "iconic architects" instead of learning more about the human; for whom we design. Two or three brief research findings about our humankind might help to clarify. Different studies revealed that our well-being is proven to be affected by the quality of the built environment[1], our decision-making is mainly relying on our intuitive feelings rather than rational thinking[2], and our cognition is actually embodied; we think with the body and not the mind[3].

Personally, I learn a lot more when I go out, explore and experience how is it like to be there on the spot observing the different artistic, architectural, and even natural elements surrounding me.

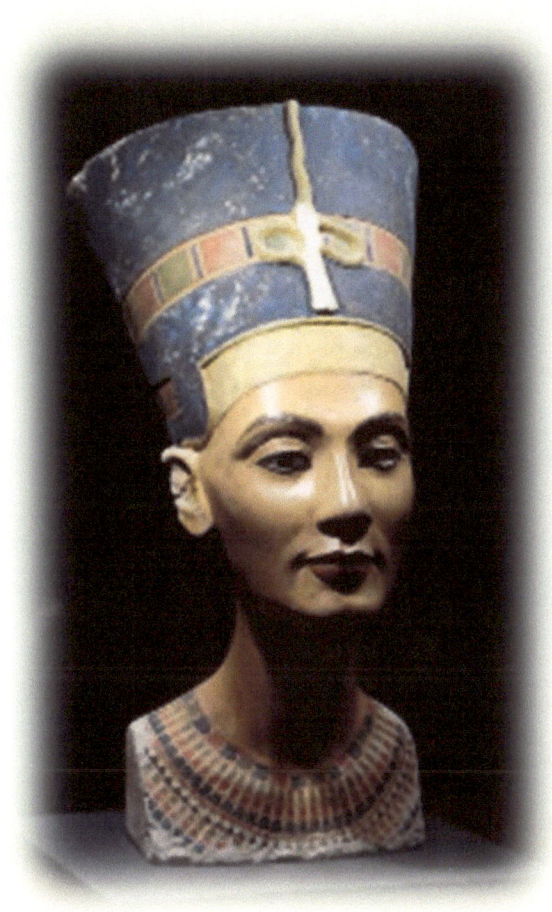

As an architect, "the more you experience, the more you learn" Steven Holl says: Hence, I owe my teachers; the creators of intriguing works of all kinds- like that of the bust of Nefertiti-what I now have come to know. Unlike what you might think, the magnificent piece is now sadly not in one of the Egyptian museums. The bust that we hope it makes it to its homeland is in the Neues Museum in Germany, where it remains as one of the masterpieces and main visitor attractions as long as the Egyptian right for ownership is continuously denied by the German authorities.

References:

1. Kellert, S.R.; Heerwagen, J. and Mador, M., 2011. Biophilic design: the theory, science and practise of bringing buildings to life. John Wiley & Sons.

2. Oppong, F., 2020. Psychologists Explain How Emotions, Not logic, Drive Human Behaviour Medium. URL https://medium.com/personal-growth/psychologists-explain-how-emotions-not-logic-drive-human-behaviour-6ed0daf76218 (accessed 2.4.21).

3. Niedenthal, P.M., 2007. Embodying emotion. science, 316(5827), pp.1002-1005.

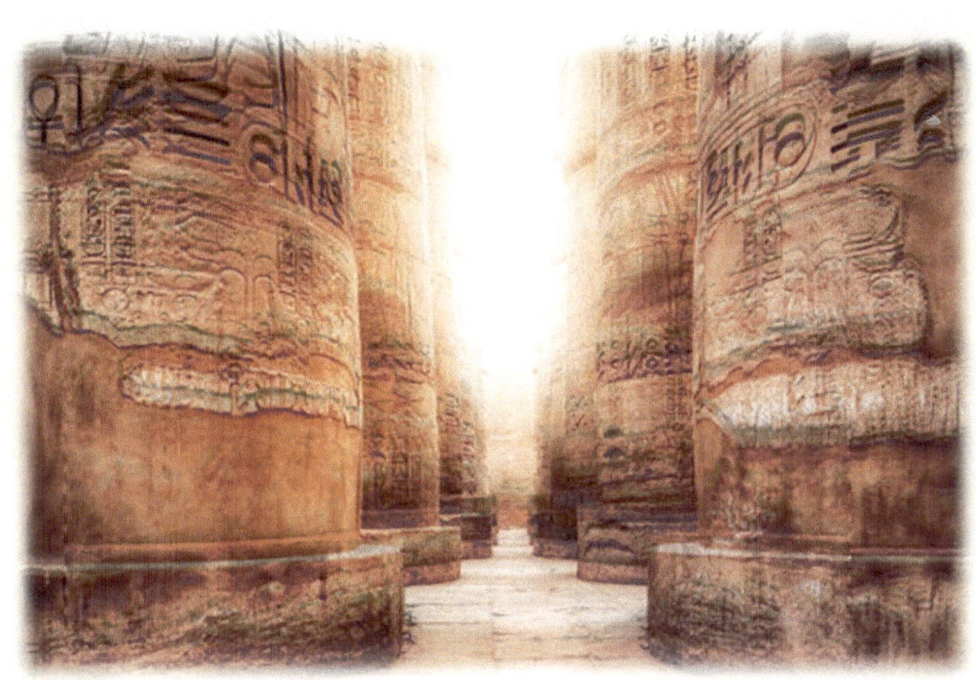

Immersive Atmospheres

They are just everywhere, your favourite restaurant, that novel you have lived in your imagination just as much as you have read, and surely that movie that you can endlessly watch again and again. When people ask me about my PhD project, they don't know that I am just as surprised as they are once I am finished explaining the often-neglected power of architecture to engage, to overwhelm and to attach by the merit of its atmosphere. They were surprised by a deep new topic, and I`m surprised because of what they tell me about how they used to think of architecture. It was then that I realized how it was pushed back to be just an abstract envelope to people nowadays, design and architecture students among them too.

It is not any more surprising to find people explaining how they fell in love with a painting, a piece of music or even a cafe they have recently been to, and sometimes they even mention the word atmosphere in their reviews, while on the other hand, when architecture students present their design projects they never get to that level of detail nor do they design for it. When I think about it further, I say to myself maybe that is how these sad-looking box buildings were born in the first place.

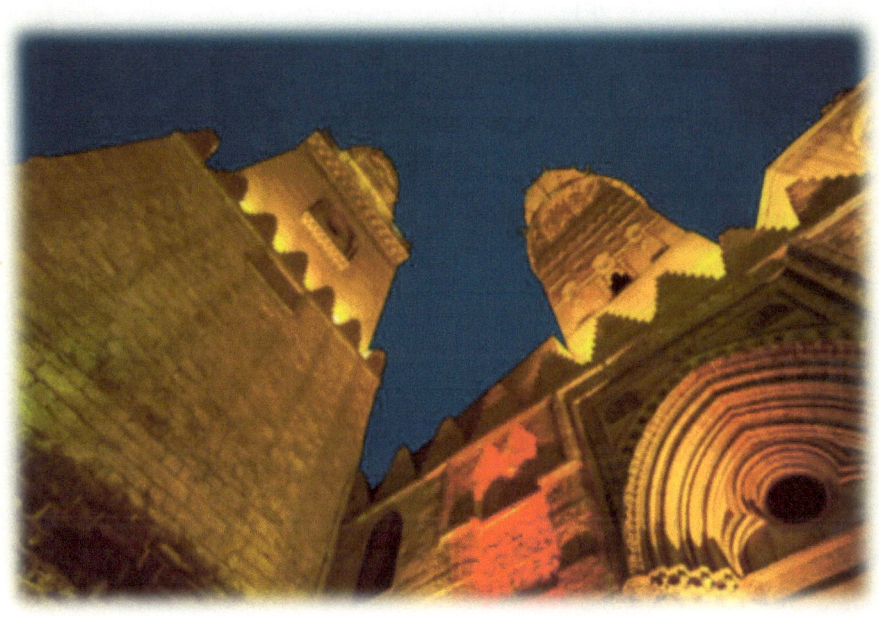

I think a little more and I find that not only the majority of modern architecture has lost its spirit but also that individual that is overly overwhelmed with smartphones, devoid activities, and abstract input that makes it even harder to appreciate, to contemplate and ultimately to truly live. After all, just as it the deep views on art that define it through its communication with the people watching; there would be no communication without both architectural works and the people, and there will be no beauty if we are not there to see it, not to mention appreciate it and make it ourselves. I remember very well how I felt as I walked into some pyramids in Egypt. I remember the awe I felt at the moment I stood right next to one of them, and it just shocked me how undeniable it was what those great designs communicated to me as I exist in them, beside them or even when looking at them. It wasn't just the pyramids that made those trips memorable, but the questions they raised as well. Standing in front of the details of one of the murals, a colleague wondered, "How come these people, humans just like us, are capable of such greatness, beauty, and human perfection when we with all this technology are incapable?!". I cannot claim that I figured all the differences between us and them at the time, but sure enough, that very question popped in my head repeatedly.

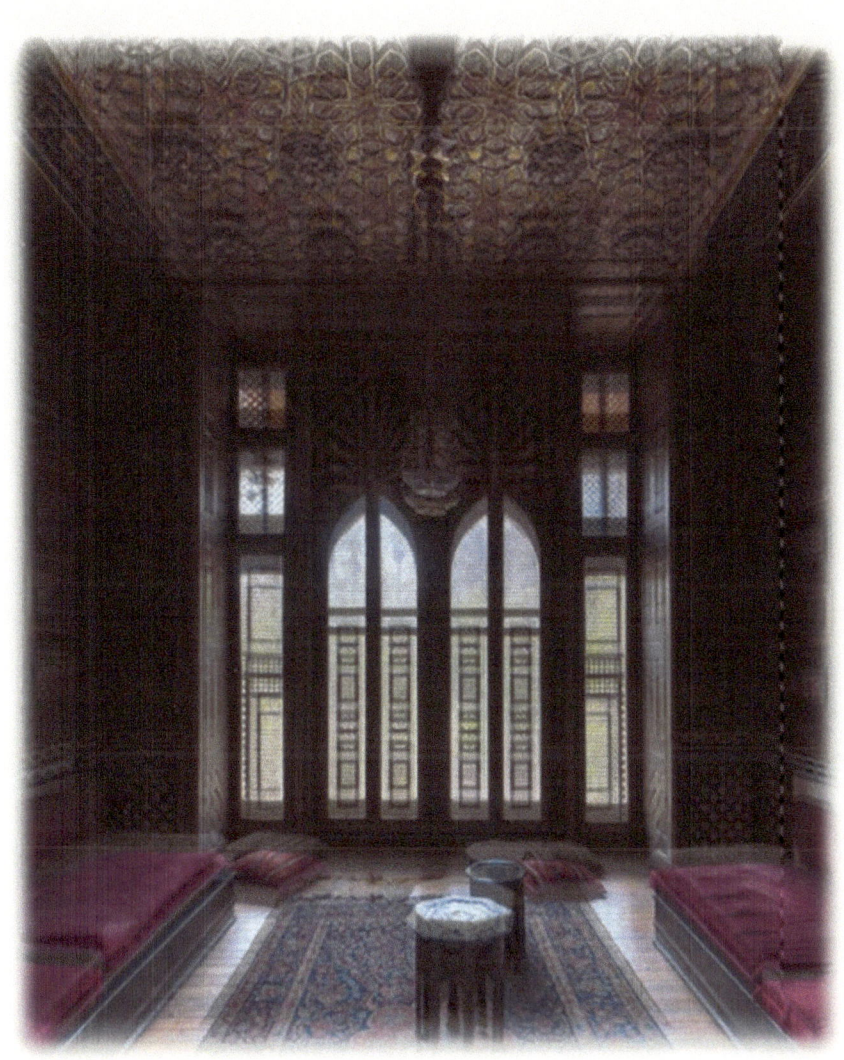

I read Pallasmaa`s argument about the importance of empathy in architecture and how even some institutions considered integrating it into architecture education, just then I thought maybe we blamed the tools too much, maybe the real dilemma is in ourselves an empathy crisis! I felt how far we have slipped every time I walked into or around an ancient building, every look I felt touching those woven ornaments of wood and stone, every taste induced by stained glass windows and mosaic domes or walls, every time I listened to the beautiful and

compassionate sound of Athan by an actual person calling for prayer while being in Al Hussain area or Al Moez street, and every time meanings were slowly revealed to me as I tried to decipher the intertwined words of poetry written in expressive Arabic calligraphy that encircled the halls in ancient mosques, Arabic houses and Turkish palaces Architecture was never an envelope, it used to be a home where all arts gather to communicate, honor and

celebrate our existence. I will also never forget how they brought tears to my eyes so easily when I came back to traveling and exploring after I had been away from them for so long.

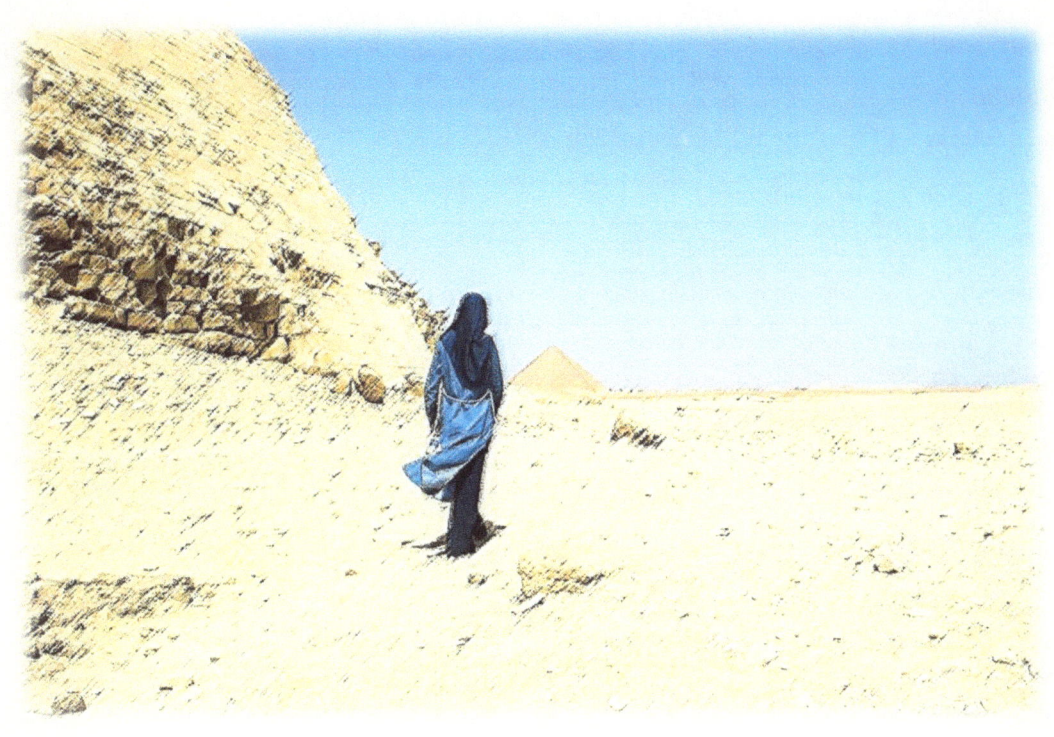

Not that they expressed any melancholy, it is just that the whole thing was so beautiful that it brushed away every bit of dust and pride that a tired, dull, and bored eye could have; especially when it was used to wonder with disappointment in the cold and rather abstract buildings and modern cities: I can almost hear you asking how such beauty makes us cry? And I'll happily tell you, that's the question I Googled that night. Fortunately, I didn't have to read a lot of scientific papers before I got to the answer on one of the open discussion platforms, a simple and honest one that I can succinctly summarize from what a young woman tried to explain; we cry when we feel a lot,....and it is beauty that makes us feel the most.

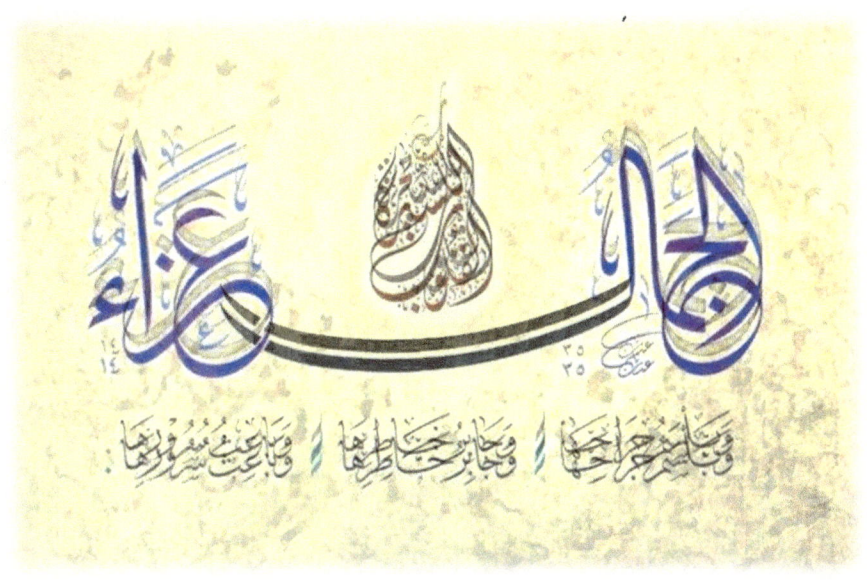

Photo after: https://www.pinterest.com/pin/355010383103135946/; last accessed:22.06.2021, 20:55. Beauty is the consolation of broken hearts, the balm of their wounds, the liberator of their mind, and the source of their joy. Arabic calligraphy: Thuluth Diwani. Calligrapher: Prof. Adnan Sheikh Othman.

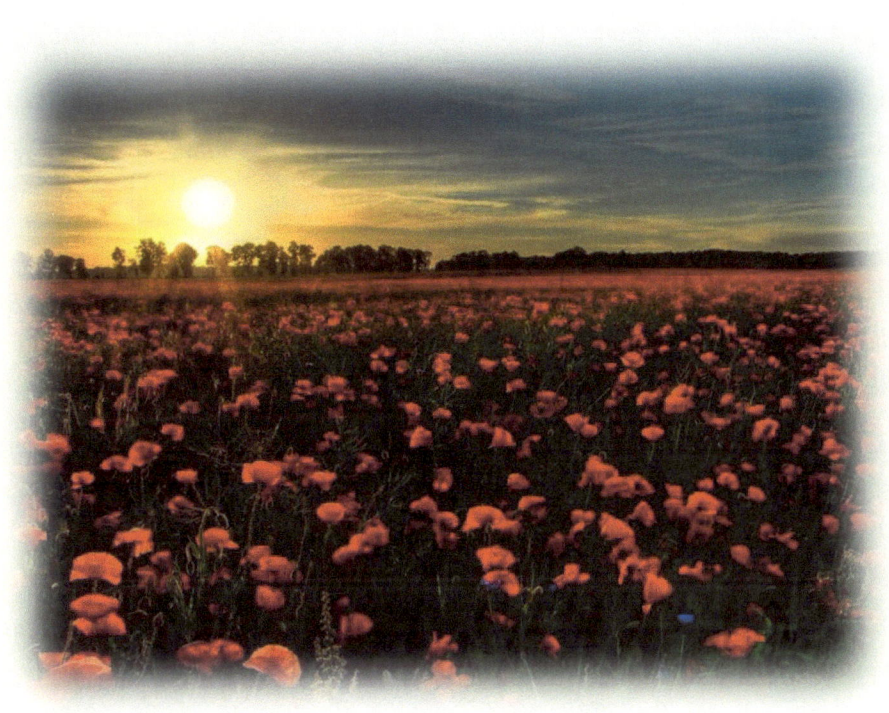

Night...that mystic

Poetry, painting and other forms of art have always been inspired by that mysterious darkness with the countless stars that night brings in its folds; In a certain way, that is quite expected considering our inquisitive human nature, but it seems that night has so much to offer more than just satisfaction to the curious minds. In a similar understanding to the poets who have always been intrigued by it; night intensifies our sense of time, intimacy and reflection.

Humans have an inherent need to dwell in both space and time just as they are hardwired to belong and seek intimacy. And the night experience provides the medium, the thought-provoking ambience, and the pace to surrender and enjoy fulfilling those implied needs, which translates into inspired feelings, ideas, and contemplation. Not only its unreachable bright stars that seem to be exclusively captured in its mystic darkness, but some plants like the night-blooming jasmine or the "night musk" as known in the Arab world also fill the air with a unique, light and soothing scent that makes memories of the place and events that it witnessed with you unforgettable. Lighting is also another element that comes in handy when setting up a night-time ambience that brings out some of the details, textures, and colours that are missed on a busy day; a vivid embodiment of the motto "less is more".

38

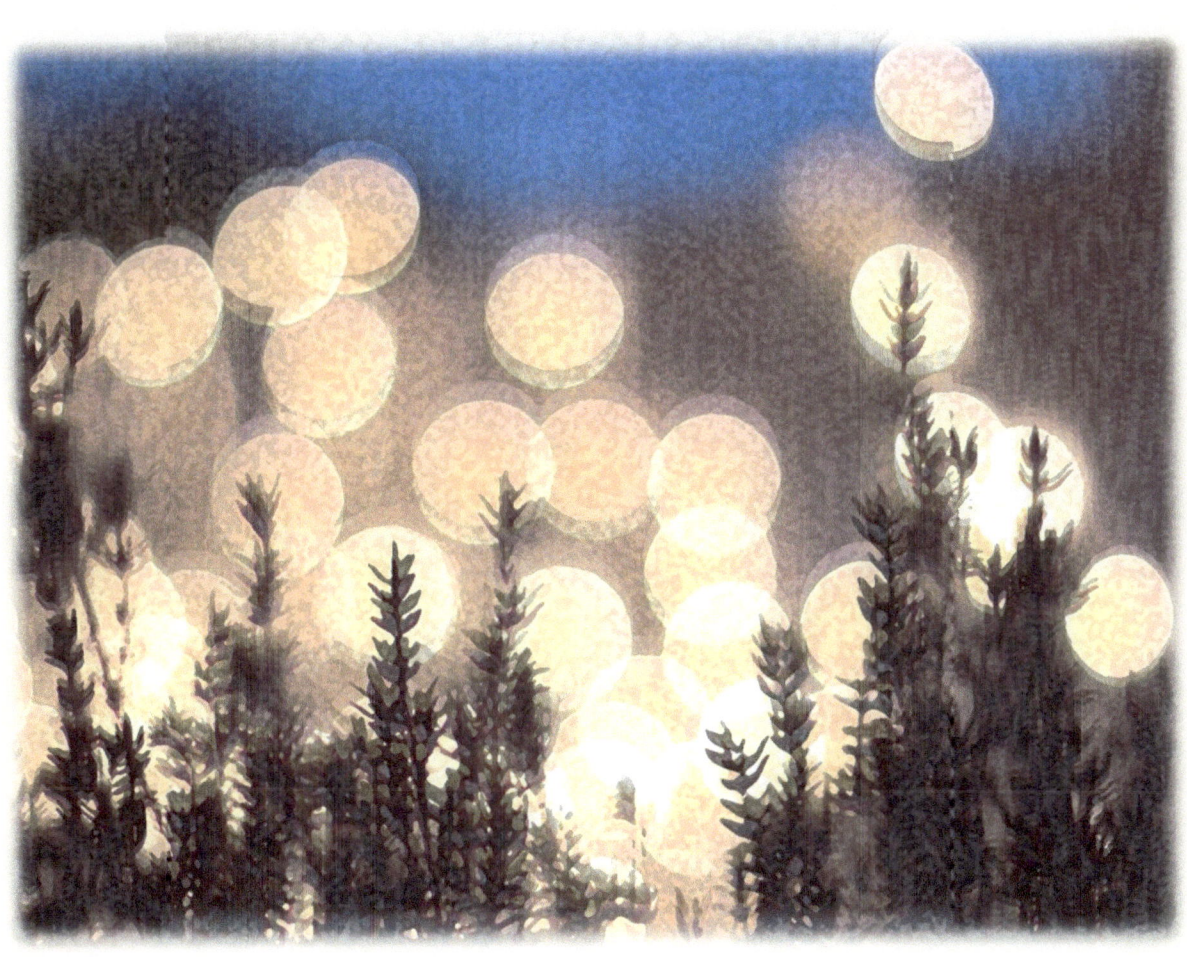

To condone the place/city experience at night is a grave sin that our existence simply refuses to forgive. Denying the human mind, body and soul the opportunity to get lost in the details of the night and its eternal horizon, and to experience its uniqueness, is just another consequence of lopsided designs that focus only on how they look instead of how they will be experienced. Such an approach is detrimental to the quality of life, human well-being and attitude. On the other hand, appreciating the power of a multisensory approach to architecture encourages a rethinking of how what and when space is experienced so as to communicate the celebration of our existence.

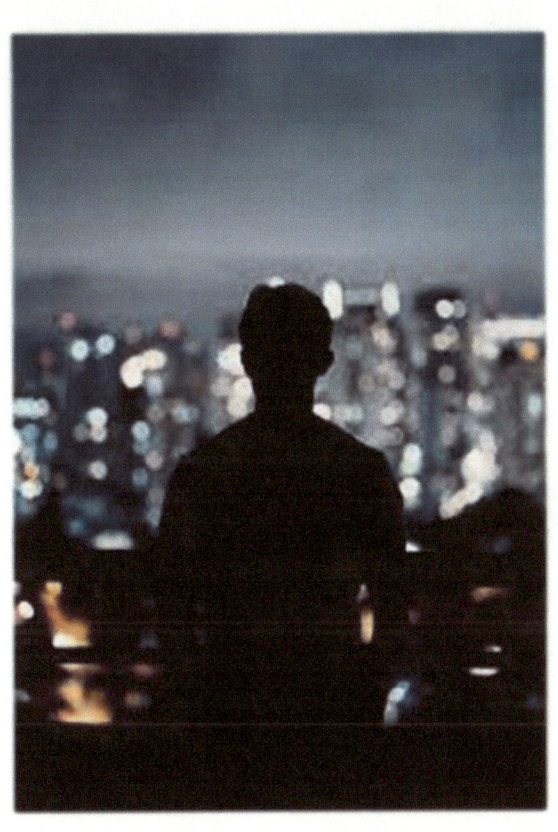

What is the point?

For those who often come from a purely scientific background like engineering, medicine or IT, it seems to be very difficult to get convinced of not only the importance of visual art (especially painting), design and architecture but also their complexity and the role they play in our daily life. They ask me while doubting the objectivity as I insist on how fundamental they are; "what is the point?". They even go as far as saying "... I mean if there is no art, the world would be pretty much the same...". Since they are also the type of people who are too busy or simply avoid investing some time having adequate exposure to good quality works or designs; I ask in my turn, isn't it also biased to judge based on an overly opinionated theory full of faulty assumptions rather than experience?

To illustrate my argument, I suggest that we begin by explaining the limitations of two points that form the basis of their perspective before moving on to the more complex aspects of the discussion. The first is a common misunderstanding of the line separating art and science, which has been discussed in the works of Pallasmaa and Peter Zumthor, clarifying the connections between neuroscience, art and architecture.

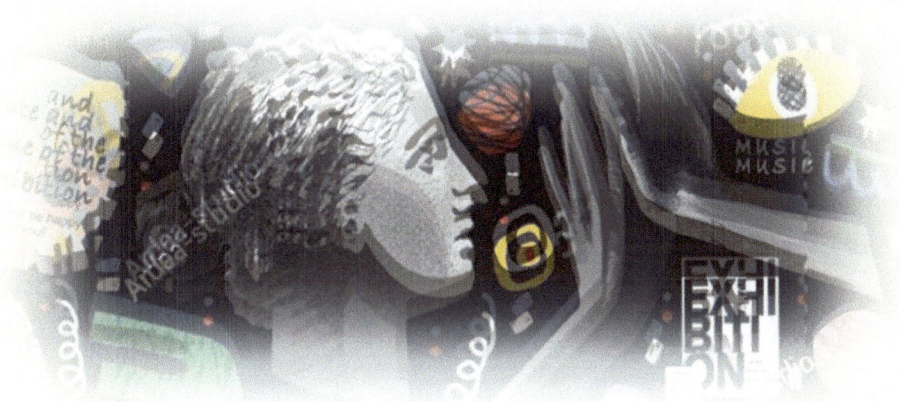

The shared areas of communication, influence and meaning in relation to the human being form the basis for their argument around the significance of "life-enhancing details" and the spirit of place that make architecture play an active and essential role on daily basis.

The second and more general point is a sense of entitlement charged with the mistaken assumption that the world in all its complexities, diversity and mystical nature can only be grasped by a single mode of logic, science, or the like. Those who had to work their way through different languages know that having a variety of languages at hand increases the ability to apprehend the world more and in different degrees and ways.

The translation is not always enough since there is a certain layer or level of meaning in one language that just cannot be put into the words of the other. A logical question to counter the advocates of singularity including those of pure logic; if one language is not enough to fully absorb or embrace the world, so how come one way in our humble minds will do?! But is it logic or is it the demand of overly simplified justification that they demand which they perhaps chose to filter what makes sense to them?!

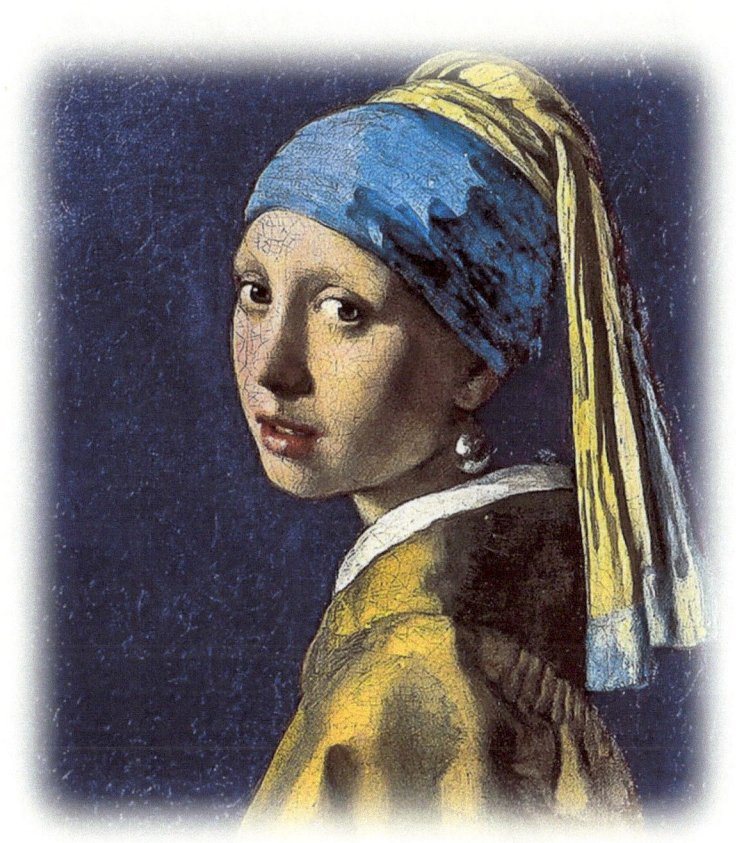

The difference that the underestimated works of art and architecture bring to our existence and experience in the world is very much the same as that of particular detail in those works. For a better explanation, I invite you to take a careful look at a couple of examples; the two paintings below are "Girl With a Pearl Earring" by Johannes Vermeer and "Tänzerin Baladine Klossowski" (Merline) by Eugen Spiro. Now imagine that the pearl erring is not in that beautifully framed painting or that the dress of the dancer in the painting on the right doesn't have the extra layer of black chiffon. Do you see the difference? Can you feel their importance?. I for one can tell another important dimension of that difference as I have also seen how dazzled the visitors of the Berlinische Galerie were, looking back and forth between the tactile model on the stand and that represented by the skilled hand which turned dense and dark paints into light, semi-transparent and delicate folds of fabric above the already dark dress in the middle of the painting.

Now that we have discussed the product, let's discuss the producer: What makes those artists put so much effort into adding that level of detail and refuse to stop before it is complete?.

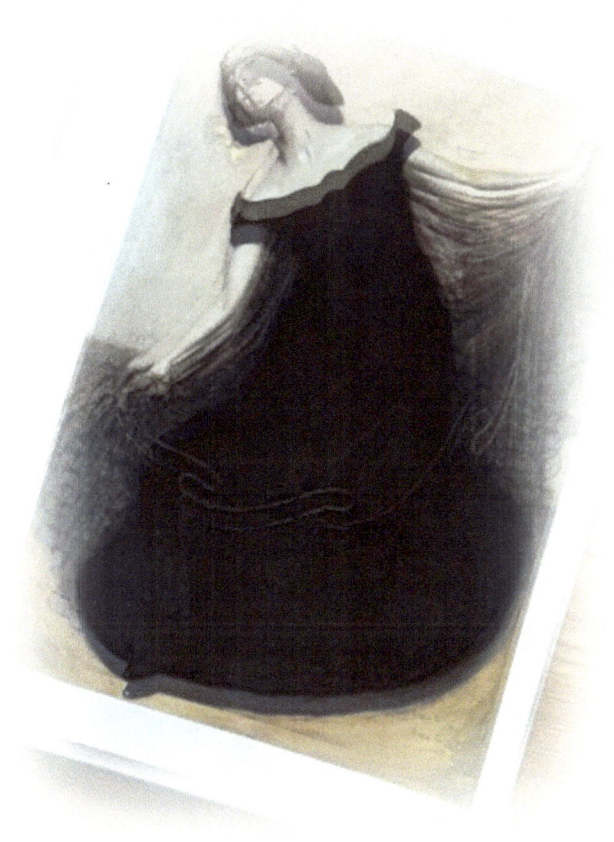

Some would argue, how about "less is more", and I understand where they are coming from but the motto should not be misused to justify poor results that come from doing less. If doing more is replaced with doing less and yet results in less ever so much, then doing more becomes even essential; in the same way that sometimes happiness can only be gained by making a vital effort. To effectively get the point across, I will explain by focusing on an extreme case of how the aforementioned professions serve an often forgotten group of the people (or persona within people). People who went through habitual burnout, trauma and depression know how hard it is to living and yet not feeling like you truly do for whatever reason that has left your view of the world brutally altered. Something more like what Germans call "Weltschmerz" or World Pain. Unlike what the majority might think, depression, for example, is not only the result of a critical change in the body's chemistry, psychology and emotional wellbeing. To be depressed is to stop seeing the beauty of this world or, to be more specific, your world. It is not necessarily due to lack of company but it is always linked to a lack of fulfilment, understanding, belonging and a desire to live that is painting your world all over with the same brush to make it even less interesting.

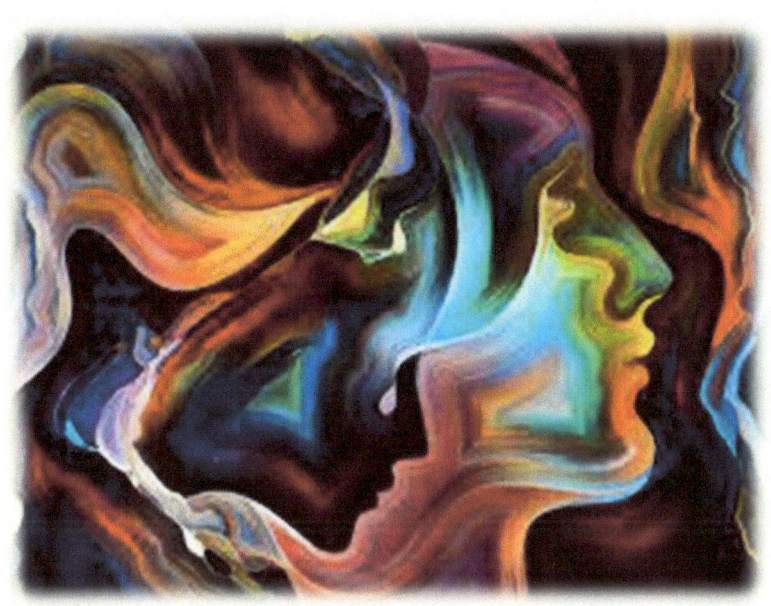

It is to push your mind to recognise the good things and yet a stubborn child in you, who has been repeatedly put off and disappointed, stands up to your face asking "What is the point?". Therefore, dealing with the mental state of a depressed person is not only a tiring process but also full of risks: Seeking treatment is certainly an essential step for recovery from depression, but the key thing on which the success of the operation depends is the tendency to rebuild that natural will to stay and stay here. Fortunately, while fixing what is in the mind is not always easy or even accessible, fixing the input that is entering the body is not just about the right diet but also the embodied perception of the world. Since the occasional arguing with the depressed is almost like a labyrinth, there is a need for some other way to make his body recognize, experience, and assimilate another view or meaning of the world; and that is exactly the power of art and architecture. Unfortunately, some of the practitioners in those disciplines themselves do not fully realise the significance of the power that distinguish the "fruits of their labour" and how the lack of successful communication reflects badly in its turn on the reputation of the stereotype spread about their professions. This vicious circle seems to begin by missing the "point" which is also particularly obvious when they allow their "labour" to be "lazy"; that is to be satisfied with their works being superficial and devoid of depth and meaning.

"The Making of the Beautiful"
"The Making of the Beautiful"

Meadow and vale and mountain,
Ocean and lake and wood
God looked on the fruit of His labor
And saw that His work was good;

And yet was there something lacking
In the world that He had made,
Something to brighten the greenness,
Something to lighten the shade.

He took a shred of the rainbow,
A bit of the sunshine's gold,
The colors of all the jewels
The mines of earth enfold.

A piece of the mist of evening
With the sunset glowing through,
A scrap of the sky at moonday,
A clear, unclouded blue;

Of these He fashioned the flowers,
And some were red, like the rose,
And some were a lovely azure,
And some were pale as the snows;

Some, shaped like a fairy chalice
The perfumed honey to hold,
And some were stars of silver,
And some were flakes of gold.

They fell in the clefts of the canyons
And high on the mountains bare,
Where never an eye should see them
Save His Who had made them fair.

His labor was not yet done;
He gathered more of the colors
Of rainbow and sky and sun,

And now unto these He added
The music of sea and land,
The tune of the rippling river,
The splash of the waves on the sand,

The raindrops' lilting measure,
The pine tree's crooning sigh,
The aspen's lisping murmur,
The wind's low lullaby,

Faint fluting of angel voices
From heavenly courts afar
And the softest, dreamiest echoes
Of the song of the morning star.

Then deftly His fingers molded
The strong and the delicate things
Lusting with the joy and the beauty
Of song and of soaring wings;

Nightingale, heron and seagull,
Bobolink, lark and then,
I think that He smiled a little
As He tilted the tail of the wren;

As He made the owl's face solemn
And twisted the blue jay's crest;
As He bent the beak of the parrot
And smoothed the oriole's best;
As He burnished the crow's jet plumage
And the robin's breast of red;
"In the cold of the northern springtime
The children will love it," He said.

So some were quaint and cunning,
And some were only funny,
And some He gave a song to,
And lo, the birds of the air.

And the snippets of things left over,
He tossed out under the skies;
Where, falling, fluttering, flying,
Behold, they were butterflies!

Those who experience depression, know all the rational answers, for example, that they are here to flourish the earth, they could even know the alarming statistics that forecast a deterioration of the planet if a decline in the number of those who under 15 years old continues but still there is always something missing. Meanwhile, reading the fantastic poem "The making of the beautiful" by Annie Johnson Flint offers another dimension to consider:

Not long after, I could not help but wonder, could this be it?!. The metaphorical picture of God`s creation similar to that of an artist in that poem made me realize that with all their uniqueness and complexities, humans to this world are just like the pearl earring in that painting. Rushing through the dictionary investigating the linguistic roots of the word "بشر ; bashar" which means human in Arabic, I found that it is indeed related to whatever is pleasing and beautiful. Only then did I realize that we are not here just to be working in this world, our existence is meant to beautify the world. It justifies a lot of other things to me, why for example, paintings of an empty desk under the tree look somewhat sad and incomplete, why the empty house or the city in lockdown is just not the same. Only I have come to know this answer, in such depth, I started truly appreciating my existence, and that is the point.

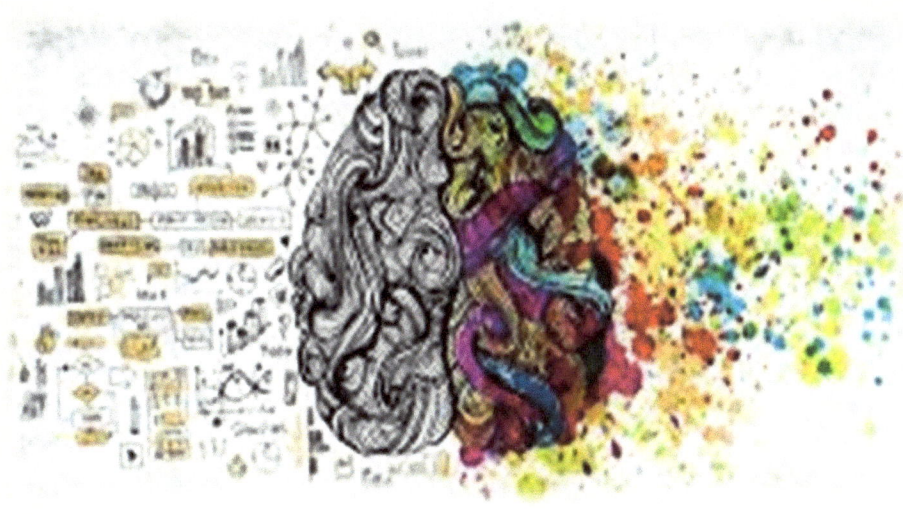

I cannot stress enough that cognition is embodied and that humans know things using their bodies and not the mind. The body is exposed directly to the qualities of these great works that communicate powerfully and beautifully. This is what helps in the healing journey for those who are struggling; an open, calm, and welcoming invitation to consider the humility of their experiences of the world by experiencing it differently. By communicating the appreciation for their existence and making them reassured that their world still has something to offer that can change the way they feel significantly so that they better experience life instead of feeling trapped; and finally realise that they still have something beautiful to offer, their world will not be the same.

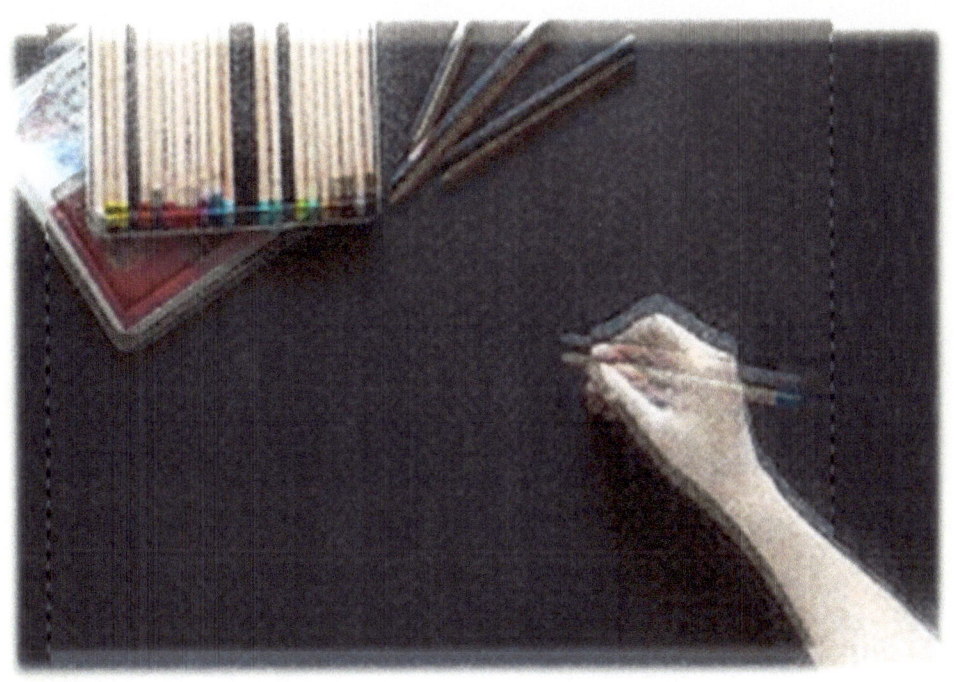

The Boring City

      Doctors have always told us to move more, go for a walk, and keep doing it as a daily habit. We, the city people try to manage to do this, but once we've decided to go outside, we all try to find our way around that 'elephant in the room'. It is kind of unfortunate that this elephant is figurative, because the problem I am trying to highlight here is what I hope we architects and planners finally acknowledge, and that is the stress of boredom in our cities.

Yes, boredom, stress and depression are not only linked to each other but also severely affect our wellbeing as recent studies have found out. I admit that our job as designers is really complex and full of different kinds of issues that we have to take into account, but on the other hand, providing a better human experience in the city should also be a top priority. A small change in how we understand, locate and choose the different elements in streets and parks can have a huge impact, if we just try to consider what it means, how it affects people and to what extent it meets their needs. The scientific definition of boredom indicates that what we aim at should be neither too easy nor too difficult if we are to avoid ending up with a boring experience.

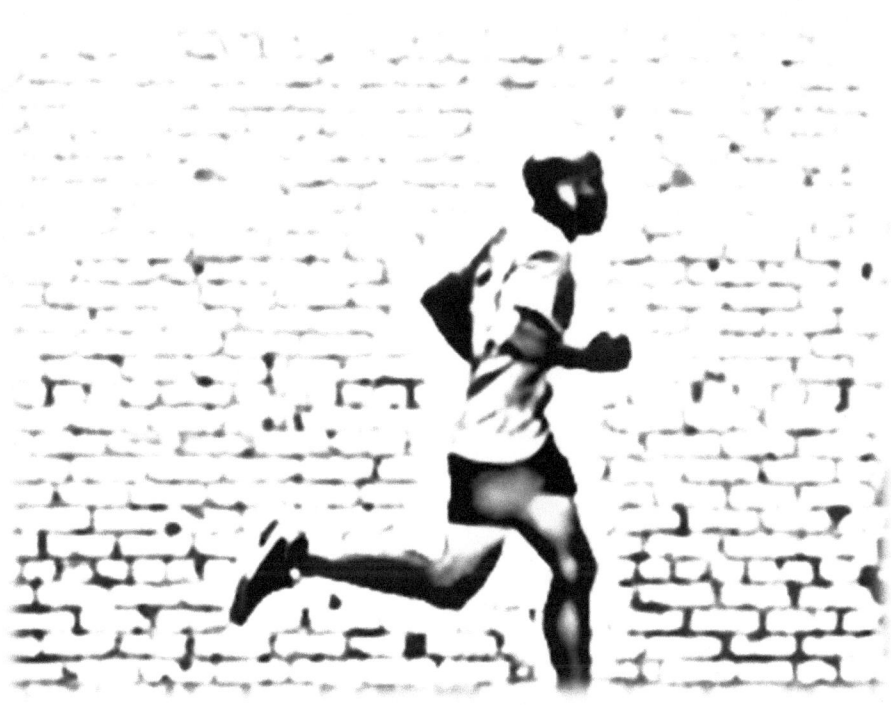

Providing a variety of experiences, including physical, sensory, cognitive, psychological and cultural, meets the natural needs of the population to learn, feel, act and interact with their surroundings.

After all, even if we ignore the consequences and continue to deny how important it is to shape a well-balanced experience in the built environment, there is still going to be an experience anyway. The fatigue that results from lack of motivation, interest, or meaning will persist and the mental and physical health of the population will continue to suffer; especially in times of lockdown when they have no other distraction from interacting with their surroundings as they go out for a breather.

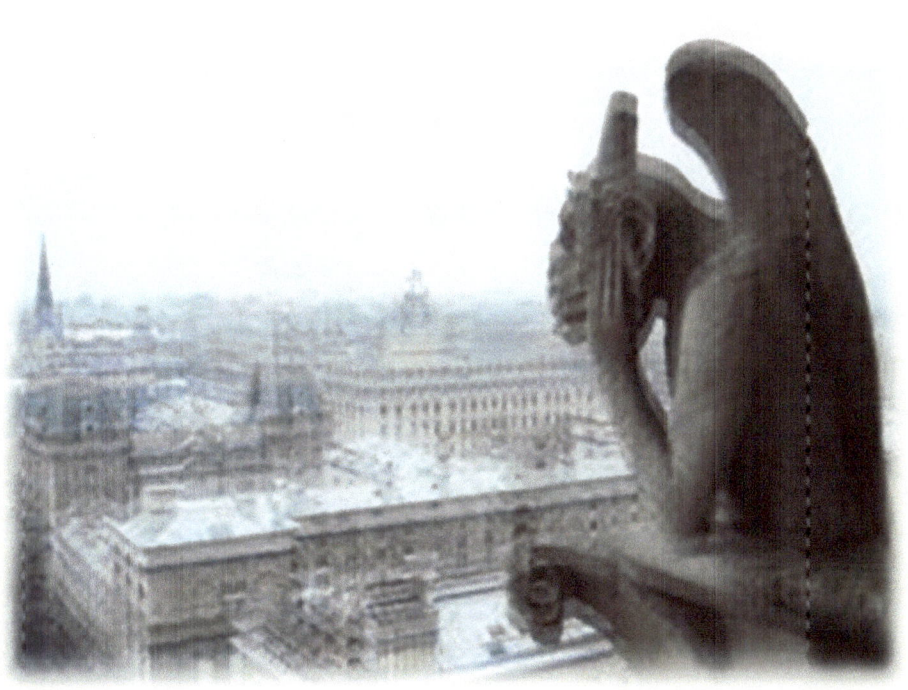

Ethics before creativity

"Justice is the basis of urbanisation" is the letteral translation of one of the famous lines of "المقدمة; Al-Muqaddimah"; "Introduction", the great book of Ibn Khaldun, the well-known ancient Arab philosopher, sociologist, and historian. However, the word that he used was not literary urbanisation. The Arabic language is well known for the nuance differences between alternatives it offers that may not simply translate into one word in other languages.

Hence, the original Arabic word "عمران;Umran" which he chose for the exact type of urbanization that results from justice reveals, is that of good quality to prosper as a civilization. Ethics and creativity are not often discussed as intertwined nor conditional in the various capacity-building programmes across the world, although they are. It seems like creativity is equally influenced by physical boundaries as studies have revealed (i.e. proportions of a room, the height of the ceiling … etc) as well as by the closer boundaries and dead ends that a lack of belief and trust deeply establishes in oneself.

For a creative mind to function there has to be not only passion but safety and trust first and foremost. Safety is not only deeply ingrained in our survival mode, but also in the necessary feeling of reassurance to invest time and effort.

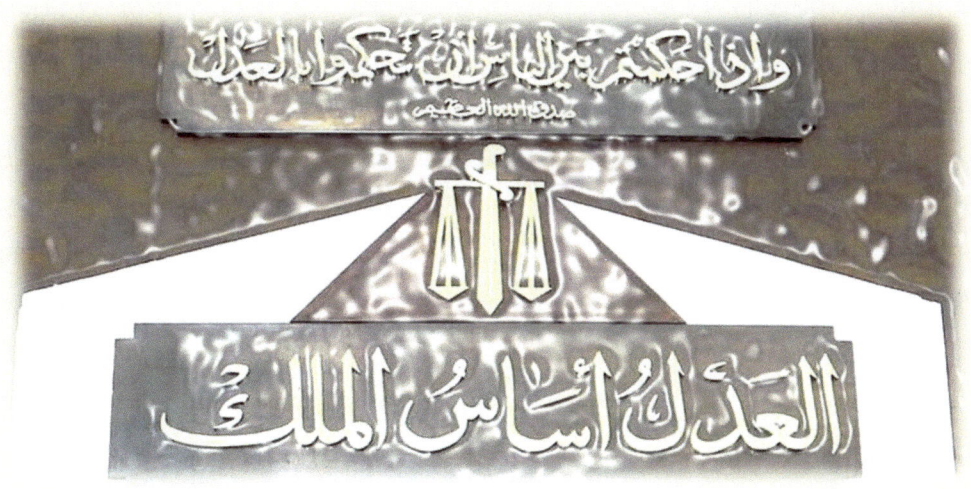

"Indeed, Allah commands you to render trusts to whom they are due and when you judge between people to judge with justice". Surat An-Nisa' [4:58] "Justice is the foundation of governance". Omar bin Abdul Aziz-Caliph of Muslims during the first century of Islam.

It is such a wise way we as creatures are designed to be selective, cautious and efficient. In an age of endless alternatives, organizations thrive to be creative enough to stand out, to keep up with the pace of development and survive their business. Yet, ethical issues continue to grow in our age and even within the same bodies striving to prosper. Perhaps because the issue of justice is unlike that of creativity; it is no more a question of doing than a question of being. It cannot unconditionally conform to practicalities of business; it is more a matter of existence. Therefore, teaching the members of a team to do something is relatively easier and probably what needs more consideration is how we teach one to be.

Ibn-Khaldun has also asserted the strong link between urbanization and justice when he reversed the relationship between the two in another famous line of his: "Injustice brings about the ruin of civilisation". The strong emphasis put on this principle since ancient times not only by the famous philosopher raises the question about our organisations nowadays; will they ever focus on more justice just as they focus on more creativity?!.

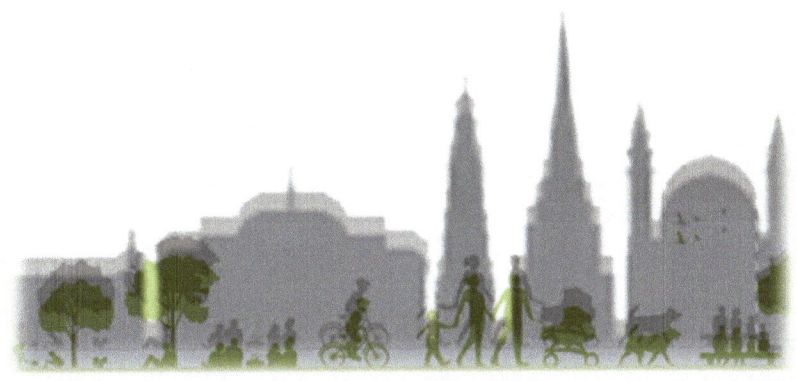

What is time?

I was wondering the other day, what is time really? How to explain it? I kept looking for answers, reading different explanations in physics, philosophy and linguistics. Then I realized that what the clock is reading the counting of the chances given in a day. The concept of time is mostly an illusion. Obviously, the minute we wake up we have to prioritize, use the chances efficiently as possible but what we are challenging really is not the counting, it is the pressure, the consequences and the outcomes of drawing these resources in certain things instead of others. I will explain; the ongoing movement of the planet in space is what is causing the changes we are influenced with here, so what we are dealing with really is how to keep up with the change, how to make use of the chances counted l the clock is just giving us a cue keep doing what we are doing or not, which is informed with our experience, limits of energy and nature.

Basically, you can freely choose to concentrate on something with the aim of producing certain results but you have to consider that there are results that you don't want too, so you get to choose wisely what and how much are you concentrating on and for what purpose.

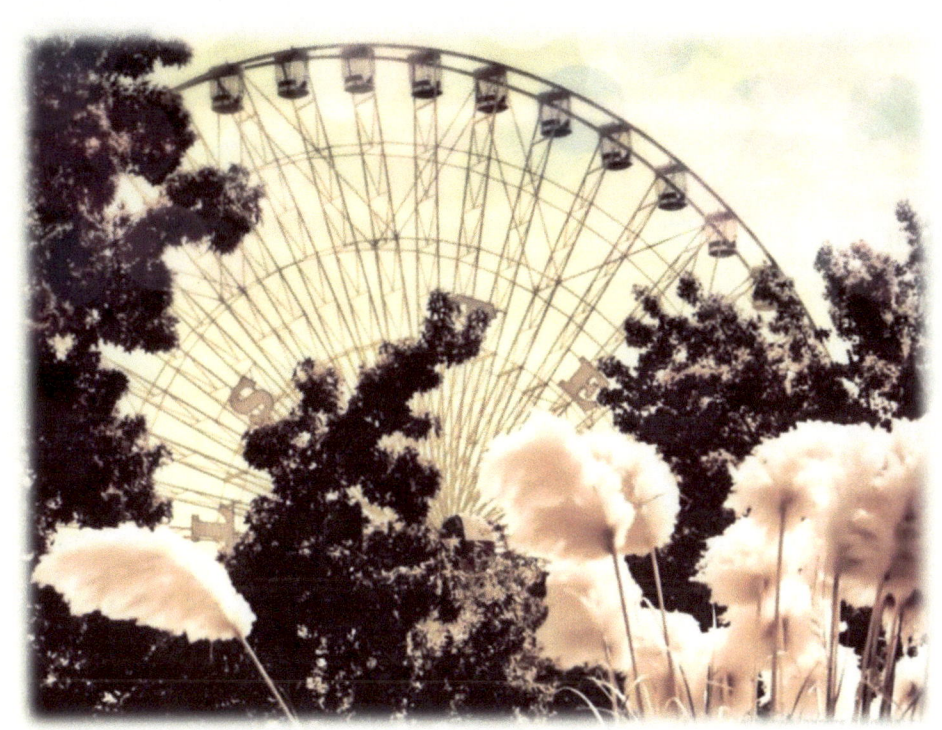

Our human nature produces self destructive behaviors when it cannot keep up with the change surrounding it, I guess it is something like a constant feeling of threat or urgent need that asks to be fulfilled, so, when you focus on the right thing in the right amount, you get more chance handling those needs and changes. See, the word for time in Arabic is "زمن;Zaman"', and in Arabic you can derive the basic origin of the noun giving a verb that you can use in different tenses, the verb here is "تزامن;tzaman" in past means resonates. What a beautiful gift to get to know different languages ha? You get another door to make sense of the world.
So, time really is not something that we own, it is one more chance given to us every year, day and second.

In love with the world

When you mention the word loneliness, people get chills in their bodies, their faces get sad and they want to change the subject in milliseconds. Actually loneliness is not dangerous, what is dangerous about loneliness is when you get desperate for the other no matter how much you actually don't like them nor the way they treat you and you escape questioning yourself... Uhhh what am I actually doing with these people?. Time does that to you. Days go by and apart from greeting the workers everywhere you walk into, you haven't got the chance to speak to sole. Up until that point, that moment of enlightenment that hits you in the face to realize that people are not the world, they are not everything and should not be as important; they are important for certain things, but not for you to live. When you fall in love with the bigger world, full of all kinds of wonder to interact with as experience, you get a bit closer to yourself as being lonely, you stop running away from that needy clingy and lonely child in you, you start loving yourself, your existence. You start parenting that child, taking him to nice places, you start tasting the food, music and beauty together, and what a nice feeling you get out of tranquillity sometimes, you get to keep it and get addicted to its presence, to say to yourself what a nice company to spend time in this world.

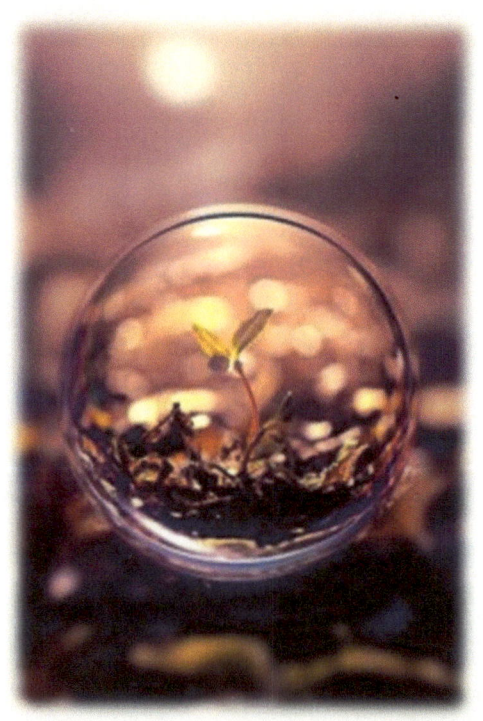

About the Author

Faten Mostafa Hatem,
an Egyptian architect, artist, and researcher. She was born and raised in Amman, Jordan.

The arguments made in this travel memoir are inspired by her experience traveling around the world from age of 15 years old as a knowledge seeker while learning different languages with a mixed background that combines science with different types of art including poetry, crafts, and painting.

She has been recently awarded two best presentations for outstanding work at the international conference "Smart Cities and Urban Analytics" in London, UK, for her work "Smart in Performance: "More to Practical Life than Hardware and Software" and "What Smart Can Learn About Art".

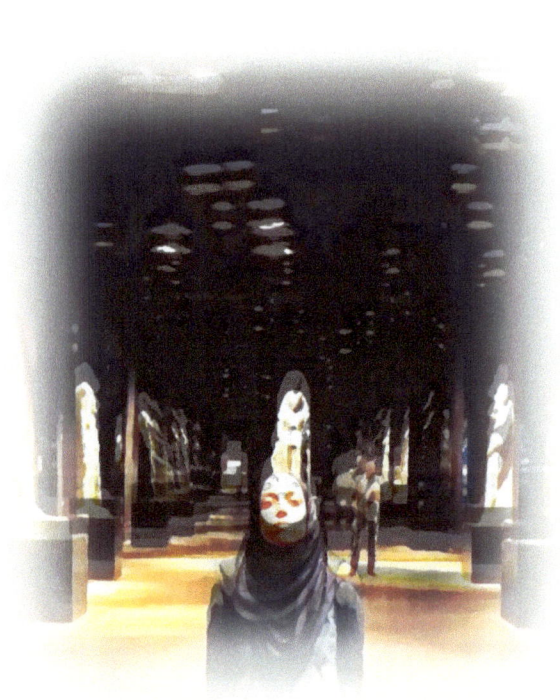

www.ingramcontent.com/pod-product-compliance
Lightning Source LLC
Chambersburg PA
CBHW051917210526
45473CB00006B/2050